Coming Home

Also by Richard Foster

Coming Home

A Prayer Journal

Created with
Richard J. Foster

HarperSanFrancisco
A Division of HarperCollins*Publishers*

Introduction

You hold in your hands what I hope will become a prayer journal—your prayer journal. It is not that now. Now it is only bound pages containing a variety of quotations from the Bible and my writings. But it is designed to nudge you toward both prayer and journal writing. And most of us need all the help we can get in both categories.

What is a "prayer journal"? Well, if prayer is the ongoing interaction we have with God, and a journal is a record of those experiences and thoughts we deem valuable, then a prayer journal preserves those interactions, events, and reflections that track our personal history with God. It is an Ebenezer of sorts—a way of declaring "hitherto has the Lord helped us."

History is replete with the prayer journals of disciples of Jesus Christ. From Augustine's *Confessions* to Lady Julian's *Showings* to Pascal's *Pensées* to Woolman's *Journal* to Dag Hammarskjöld's *Markings* to Luci Shaw's *God in the Dark,* we are privileged to share in some of the finest of Christian devotion. These journals, of course, are but a small sampling of the myriad upon myriad of unpublished prayer journals of followers of the Way throughout the centuries. It is a long and honored tradition.

Question: What do you do with a prayer journal? Answer: Almost anything you want. There is no right way or wrong way to go about keeping a prayer journal. You are a unique individual before God, with special gifts that only God can reveal and special needs that only God can satisfy. Together, you and God will find the prayer and journal pilgrimage that is best for you.

Having said this, it still might be useful to you if I make a few general remarks. I encourage you, first of all, to comment freely on the events of your day. This differs from notations in a diary by its focus on why and wherefore, rather than who and what. The external events are springboards for understanding God's deeper workings in the heart. Perhaps a particular encounter stirs up feelings of anger and defensiveness in you, or maybe pride and hope. Why? What is God teaching you through this experience? Remember, God's scrutiny is a scrutiny of love.

As you write, you will discover times when finding just the right word or phrase becomes important. You might begin with a prayer such as, "Jesus, teach me your love." But as the process of prayer leads you deeper into the reality you are seeking, you will notice the prayer changing ever so slightly—and profoundly: "Lord, let me enter your love," or maybe "Jesus, let me receive your embrace."

So when seeking to experience prayer, I think it is wise to allow plenty of space for crossing things out, adding commentary, drawing arrows or other scribbles, and so forth. The same holds true if you are writing poetry—even more so. Time spent discovering the right word or phrase that gives voice to your heart cry is never time wasted.

You may even want to set aside a page for a particular prayer or poem and date each time you return to it, making revisions, notes, or additional thoughts.

On the other hand, it is important not to get too tangled up in words. Sometimes it is best to let thoughts tumble forth unedited and uncensored. You may want to write by means of free association or stream of consciousness. (Sometimes I like to doodle!) Throughout, be open to Divine surprises—new ways of seeing, thinking, hearing, feeling.

At times, when I am praying for another, I will place that person's name at the top of the page and then prayerfully begin to sketch out a picture. Perhaps a tree with roots going down deep and strong branches reaching skyward. Perhaps a rose opening up to the sunlight. Perhaps a wall of protection surrounding the person. Whatever. And my little picture becomes my prayer on behalf of another.

Now, a word about the various quotations scattered throughout this prayer journal. I hope these will serve as signposts on your journey where you can pause and ponder. As you respond to the idea expressed on the page, you may find your thoughts going in new and unexpected directions. Good. For example, as you contemplate Elizabeth Fry's tender prayer, "O Lord! enable me to be more and more, singly, simply, and purely obedient to thy service," you may well be drawn into clearer resolves for yourself. Or maybe into prayers of your own. Or simply into stillness. In whatever direction you are led, I would urge you to follow these gentle and powerful movements of Grace.

Above all, a prayer journal has a way of focusing, clarifying, keeping us honest. Self-centered prayers become manifestly so when committed to paper—even to us, their authors. Insights that seem like hazy figures on our horizon sometimes become crystal clear when written down. Vacillating indecision sometimes turns into marching orders.

So, I commend you to God as you begin this prayer journal. Who knows? Perhaps, just perhaps, through the process of prayer journal writing you will, like Moses, catch a glimpse of the backside of God. But even if you see nothing and hear nothing, you can still rest assured that you too are hidden in the cleft of the rock.

Richard J. Foster

We are exiles
and aliens
until we can
come into
God, the
heart's true
home.

"Lord, teach
us to pray."
—*Luke 11:1*

Begin by inviting God to kindle
a fire of love within you.

The truth is that
we only learn to
pray all the time
everywhere after
we have resolutely
set about praying
some of the time
somewhere.
—*John Dalrymple*

We will never have pure enough motives, or be good enough, or know enough in order to pray rightly. We simply must set all these things aside and begin praying.

"If my people who
are called by my
name humble
themselves, pray,
seek my face, and
turn from their
wicked ways, then
I will hear from
heaven, and will
forgive their sin and
heal their land."
—*2 Chronicles 7:14*

Pray as you can,
not as you can't.
—*Dom Chapman*

Real
prayer
is life
creating
and life
changing.

Your prayer must be
turned inwards, not
towards a God of
Heaven nor towards a
God far off, but
towards God who is
closer to you than you
are aware.
—*Anthony Bloom*

It is the Discipline of prayer
that brings us into the
deepest and highest work
of the human spirit.

Then Jesus
told them a
parable about
their need to
pray always
and not to
lose heart.
—*Luke 18:1*

It is not a journey
into ourselves
that we are
undertaking, but
a journey *through*
ourselves so that
we can emerge
from the deepest
level of the self
into God.

To pray means
to be willing
to be naive.
—*Emilie Griffin*

In prayer, real
prayer, we begin
to think God's
thoughts after
him: to desire the
things he desires,
to love the things
he loves, to will
the things he
wills.

Find the door of
your heart, you
will discover it is
the door of the
Kingdom of God.
—*John Chrysostom*

To believe
that God can
reach us and
bless us in the
ordinary
junctures of
daily life is
the stuff of
prayer.

Do not worry about anything, but in everything
by prayer and supplication with thanksgiving let
your requests be made known to God.
—*Philippians 4:6*

Humility means to
live as close to the
truth as possible: The
truth about ourselves,
the truth about
others, the truth
about the world in
which we live.

Today, this very
moment, Jesus is
inviting you, Jesus is
inviting me, into his
rest: "Take my yoke
upon you, and learn
from me, for I am
gentle and humble
 in heart, and you
will find rest for
your souls."
—*Matthew 11:29*

We must learn
holy listening. We
are listening,
always listening,
for the Divine
Whisper amid the
human clatter.

What we need is a
desire to know the
whole will of God,
with a fixed
resolution to do it.
—*John Wesley*

To pray is to
change.
Prayer is the
central
avenue God
uses to
transform us.

God thirsts to
be thirsted after.
—*Augustine*

We do not have to have
everything perfect
when we pray. The
Spirit reshapes, refines,
and reinterprets our
feeble, ego-driven
prayers. We can rest in
this work of the Spirit
on our behalf.

To set the mind on
the flesh is death,
but to set the mind
on the Spirit is life
and peace.
—*Romans 8:6*

You who live in the shelter of
        the Most High,
who abide in the shadow of the
        Almighty
will say to the LORD, "my
        refuge
and my fortress;
my God, in whom I trust."

—*Psalm 91:1–2*

Help me to
walk in your
steps. Teach me
to see only
what you see,
to say only
what you say,
to do only what
you do. Help
me, Lord, to
work resting
and to pray
resting.

For thus said the
Lord GOD, the
Holy One of
Israel: In
returning and
rest you shall be
saved; in
quietness and in
trust shall be
your strength.
—*Isaiah 30:15*

I do desire to
come into
harmony with
you more fully
and more often. I
do desire a
fellowship that is
constant and
sustaining. Please
nurture this desire
of mine.

Progress in
intimacy with
God means
progress toward
silence. "For God
alone my soul
waits in silence,"
declares the
Psalmist in
Psalm 62:1.

Love is the
response of the
heart to the
overwhelming
goodness of God,
so come in
simply and speak
to him in
unvarnished
honesty.

God loves you, is
present in you,
lives in you,
dwells in you,
calls you, saves
you, and offers
you an
understanding
and light which
are like nothing
you ever found in
books or heard in
sermons.
—*Thomas Merton*

My Lord and
my God,
listening is hard
for me. . . . I
need your help
if I am to be
still and listen.
I would like to
try. . . . Help me
to try now.

Do not forget that
the value and
interest of life is not
so much to do
conspicuous things
. . . as to do ordinary
things with the
perception of their
enormous value.
—*Teilhard de Chardin*

We may not see the end from the beginning, but we keep on doing what we know to do. We pray, we listen, we worship, we carry out the duty of the present moment.

For I will restore
health to you, and
your wounds I will
heal, says the Lord.
—*Jeremiah 30:17*

We will never *have*
time for prayer—
we must *make* time.

"Far be it from me that I should sin against the LORD by ceasing to pray for you."
—*1 Samuel 12:23*

All good work is
pleasing to the Father.
Even the jobs that seem
meaningless and
mindless to us are
highly valued in the
order of the Kingdom
of God. God values the
ordinary.

Everything that
one turns in the
direction of God
is prayer.
—*Ignatius of Loyola*

Waiting itself becomes prayer as we give our waiting to God. In waiting we begin to get in touch with the rhythms of life—stillness and action, listening and decision. They are the rhythms of God. It is in the everyday and the commonplace that we learn patience, acceptance, and contentment.

"Holy, holy, holy, the Lord God the Almighty,
who was and is to come."
—*Revelation 4:8*

Help me to
be a conduit
through
which your
healing love
can flow to
others.

We pursue God because
and only because He
has first put an urge
within us that spurs us
to the pursuit.
—*A. W. Tozer*

Each day in a new and living way the brooding Spirit of God teaches us. As we begin to follow these nudgings of the Spirit, we are changed from the inside out.

"Ask, and it will
be given you;
search, and you
will find; knock,
and the door will
be opened for
you."
—*Matthew 7:7–8*

Love loves to
be told what
it knows
already. . . . It
wants to be
asked for
what it longs
to give.
—*P. T. Forsyth*

Forgiveness
means that the
power of love
that holds us
together is
greater than the
power of the
offense that
separates us.

"I give you a new commandment, that you love one another. Just as I have loved you, you also should love one another. By this everyone will know that you are my disciples, if you have love for one another."

—*John 13:34–35*

If we truly
love people,
we will desire
for them far
more than it is
within our
power to give
them, and this
will lead us to
prayer.
Intercession is
a way of
loving others.

Beloved, if our hearts do not
condemn us, we have boldness
before God; and we receive from
him whatever we ask, because we
obey his commandments and do
what pleases him.
—*1 John 3:21–22*

When in honesty
we accept the evil
that is in us as part
of the truth about
ourselves and offer
that truth up to
God, we are in a
mysterious way
nourished. Even
the truth about
our shadow side
sets us free.

There is no
mode of life in
the world more
pleasing and
more full of
delight than
continual
conversation
with God.
—*Brother Lawrence*

How great are
your works,
O LORD! Your
thoughts are
very deep!
—*Psalm 92:5*

Let us be among those who believe that
the inner transformation of our lives is a
goal worthy of our best effort.

There is no stage of prayer so
sublime that it isn't necessary to
return often to the beginning.
—*Teresa of Avila*

Holy prayers are
needed in order to
dream new dreams
and see new visions.

When I give thanks, my thoughts still circle about myself to some extent. But in praise my soul ascends to self-forgetting adoration, seeing and praising only the majesty and power of God, His grace and redemption.
—*Ole Hallesby*

Adoration is the
spontaneous
yearning of the
heart to worship,
honor, magnify,
and bless God.

Praise the LORD!
Praise the LORD,
O my soul! I will
praise the LORD as
long as I live; I will
sing praises to my
God all my life long.
—*Psalm 146:1–2*

We are working with God to determine the future! Certain things will happen in history if we pray rightly. We are to change the world by prayer.

"Come to me,
all you that are
weary and are
carrying heavy
burdens, and I
will give you
rest."
—*Matthew 11:28*

If we cannot find
God in the
routines of home
and shop, then
we will not find
him at all.

If prayer is the
heart of religion,
then petition is
the heart of
prayer.
—*Herbert Farmer*

As a mother comforts her child,
so I will comfort you.
—*Isaiah 66:13*

God is good and is out
to do us good always.
That gives us hope to
believe that we are the
winners, regardless of
what we are being
called upon to
relinquish. God is
inviting us deeper in
and higher up.

O Lord! enable me to be
more and more, singly,
simply, and purely
obedient to thy service.
—*Elizabeth Fry*

We are responsible
before God to pray
for those God
brings into our
circle of nearness.

You do not have,
because you do not
ask. You ask and
do not receive,
because you ask
wrongly, in order
to spend what you
get on your
pleasures.
—*James 4:2–3*

As we carry on the
business of the day,
inwardly we keep
pressing in toward
the Divine Center.
At every opportunity
we place our mind
before God with
inward confessions
and petitions.

I will give thanks
to the LORD with
my whole heart.
—*Psalm 9:1*

Be silent, and listen
to God. Let your
heart be in such a
state of preparation
that his Spirit may
impress upon you
such virtues as will
please him. Let all
within you listen to
him. This silence of
all outward and
earthly affection and
of human thoughts
within us is essential
if we are to hear his
voice.
—*Francois Fenelon*

God wants us
to be present
where we are.
He invites us
to see and to
hear what is
around us and,
through it all,
to discern the
footprints of
the Holy.

Whether you eat or drink, or whatever you do,
do everything for the glory of God.
—*1 Corinthians 10:31*

We glorify
God in our
labor because
we most
closely
approximate
the Creator
when we
engage in the
creative
activity of
work.

Whether we like
it or not, asking is
the rule of the
Kingdom.
—*C. H. Spurgeon*

A part of our
petition must
always be for an
increasing
discernment so
that we can see
things as God
sees them.

Search me,
O God, and
know my heart;
test me and
know my
thoughts. See if
there is any
wicked way in
me, and lead me
in the way
everlasting.
—*Psalms 139:23–24*

The true
prophetic
message always
calls us to
stretch our
arms out wide
and embrace
the whole
world. In holy
boldness we
cover the earth
with the grace
and the mercy
of God.

Father, I abandon
myself into your
hands; do with
me what you will.
Whatever you
may do, I thank
you: I am ready
for all, I accept
all. Let only your
will be done in
me, and in all
your creatures—
I wish no more
than this, O Lord.
—*Charles de
Foucauld*

I thank my God
through Jesus Christ
for all of you.
—*Romans 1:8*

Just as you do not
analyze the words of
someone you love, but
accept them as they
are said to you, accept
the Word of Scripture
and ponder it in your
heart, as Mary did.
That is all. That is
meditation.
—*Dietrich Bonhoeffer*

O Holy Spirit of
God, so many
hurt today. Help
me to stand with
them in their
suffering. . . .
Show me the
pathway into
their pain.

Let your suffering
be borne for God;
suffer with
submission and
patience and suffer
in union with
Jesus Christ and
you will be
offering a most
excellent prayer.
—*Jean-Nicholas Grou*

Gracious Holy Spirit, so much of my life seems to revolve around my interests and my welfare. I would like to live just one day in which everything I did benefited someone besides myself. Perhaps prayer for others is a starting point. Help me to do so without any need for praise or reward.

The Spirit helps
us in our
weakness; for we
do not know how
to pray as we
ought, but that
very Spirit
intercedes with
sighs too deep
for words.
—*Romans 8:26*

We pray, and
yet it is not we
who pray, but a
Greater who
prays in us.
—*Thomas Kelly*

I am tired of
praying. I am tired
of asking. I am tired
of waiting. But I
will keep on
praying and asking
and waiting
because I have
nowhere else to go.

"Not my
will but yours
be done."
—*Luke 22:42*

We shall come one day to a heaven where we shall
gratefully know that God's great refusals were sometimes
the true answers to our truest prayer.
—*P. T. Forsyth*

Our task in reality is
a small one: to hold
the agony of others
just long enough for
them to let go of it
for themselves.
Then together we
can give all things
over to God.

Rest. Rest. Rest
in God's love.
The only work
you are required
now to do is
to give your
most intense
attention to His
still, small voice
within.

—*Madame Guyon*

Prayer makes our
love flow freely,
both vertically and
horizontally. As we
pray, we are drawn
into the love of
God, which
irresistibly leads us
to our neighbor.
When we try to
love our neighbor,
we discover our
utter inability to do
so, which irresistibly
drives us back
to God.

We must repeat
the same
supplications
not twice or three
times only, but
as often as
we have need,
a hundred and a
thousand times. . . .
We must never be
weary in waiting
for God's help.
—*John Calvin*

We throw
caution to the
wind and pray
not just for
individuals but
also for nations,
not just for the
renewal of the
Church but
also for the
transformation
of the world. We
pray for and
work for the
Kingdom
to come on
earth—on all
the earth—as it
is in heaven.

Know that it is by
silence that the
saints grew, that
it was because of
silence that the
power of God
dwelt in them,
because of silence
that the mysteries
of God were
known to them.

—*Ammonas*

Our prayer, to the extent that it is fully authentic, undermines the status quo. It is a spiritual underground resistance movement.

The apostles said to
the Lord, "Increase
our faith!" The
Lord replied, "If
you had faith the
size of a mustard
seed, you could say
to this mulberry
tree, 'Be uprooted
and planted in the
sea,' and it would
obey you."
—*Luke 17:5–6*

To clasp the
hands in prayer is
the beginning of
an uprising
against the
disorder of the
world.
—*Karl Barth*

May you now, by the power of the Holy Spirit, receive the spirit of prayer. May it become, in the name of Jesus Christ, the most precious occupation of your life. And may the God of all peace strengthen you, bless you, and give you joy.

Sources

John Dalrymple, *Simple Prayer* (Wilmington, DE: Michael Glazier, 1984), p. 13.

Anthony Bloom, *Beginning to Pray* (New York: Paulist, 1970), p. 49.

Emile Griffin, *Clinging: The Experience of Prayer* (San Francisco: Harper & Row, 1984), p. 5.

John Crysostom as quoted in Anthony Bloom, *Beginning to Pray* (New York: Paulist, 1970), p. 46.

Augustine, as quoted in Mary Clare Vincent, *The Life of Prayer and the Way to God* (Still River, MS: St. Bede's Publications, 1982), p. 25.

Thomas Merton, *The Hidden Ground of Love*, ed. William Shannon (New York: Farrar, Straus & Giroux, 1985), p. 156.

Ignatius of Loyola as quoted in Gloria Hutchinson, *Six Ways to Pray from Six Great Saints* (Cincinnati, OH: St. Anthony Messenger Press, 1982), p. 62.

A. W. Tozer, *The Pursuit of God* (Harrisburg, PA: Christian Publications, n.d.), p. 11.

P. T. Forsyth, *The Soul of Prayer* (Grand Rapids, MI: Eerdmans, 1916), p. 63.

Brother Lawrence, *The Practice of the Presence of God* (Philadelphia: Judson, n.d.), p. 60.

Teresa of Avila, *The Collected Works of St. Teresa of Avila*, trans. Kieran Kavanaugh and Otilio Rodriguez (Washington, DC: ICS Publications, 1976), p. 94.

Ole Hallesby, *Prayer*, trans. Clarence J. Carlsen (Minneapolis, MN: Augsburg, 1959), p. 141.

H. H. Farmer, *The World and God* (London: Nisbet, 1935), p. 129.

Elizabeth Fry as quoted in *Friends of Jesus Community Newsletter 1,* no. 5 (Dec. 1990).

Francois Fenelon as quoted in Richard J. Foster, *Meditative Prayer* (Downers Grove, IL: InterVarsity, 1983), pp. 21–22.

Charles de Foucauld as quoted in Roger Pooley and Philip Seddon, eds and comps., *The Lord of the Journey: A Reader in Christian Spirituality* (San Francisco: Collins Liturgical in USA, 1986), p. 292.

Dietrich Bonhoeffer, *The Way to Freedom* (New York: Harper & Row, 1966), p. 59.

Jean-Nicholas Grou, *How to Pray*, trans. Joseph Dalby (Greenwood, SC: Attic, 1982), p. 83.

Thomas Kelly, *A Testament of Devotion* (New York: Harper & Row, 1941), p. 45.

P. T. Forsyth, *The Soul of Prayer* (Grand Rapids, MI: Eerdmans, 1916), p. 14.

John Calvin, *Sermons on the Epistle to the Ephesians* (Edinburgh, Scotland: Banner of Truth Trust, 1975), p. 683.

Ammonas as quoted in Thomas Merton, *Contemplative Prayer* (Garden City, NY: Doubleday/Image, 1971), p. 42.